The Library of
E-Commerce and Internet Careers

Careers
in
E-Commerce
Security
and
Encryption

Chris Hayhurst

The Rosen Publishing Group,
New York

Published in 2001 by The Rosen Publishing Group, Inc.
29 East 21st Street, New York, NY 10010

Library of Congress Cataloging-in-Publication Data

Hayhurst, Chris.
Careers in e-commerce security and encryption / by Chris
Hayhurst. — 1st ed.
p. cm. — (Library of e-commerce and Internet careers)
Includes bibliographical references.
ISBN 0-8239-3420-9 (library binding)
1. Computer networks—Security measures—Vocational guidance—Juvenile literature. 2. Data encryption (Computer science)—Juvenile literature. [1. Computer security. 2. Computer
security—Vocational guidance. 3. Vocational guidance.] I. Title.
II. Series.
TK5105.59 .H38 2001
658.8'4—dc21

                                                          2001000037

Manufactured in the United States of America

Table of Contents

Introduction

*I*n the late 1990s, banking giant Citibank discovered a disappearance of funds in one client account. Where could half a million dollars go overnight? Bank officials were frantic. Over the next three months, missing funds were reported sixteen more times. The thieves were transferring money from the accounts of some of the world's wealthiest people. As bank officials were used to seeing large amounts of money move in and out of these accounts, no one noticed that unauthorized activity was taking place until it was too late.

Always one step behind the criminals, the authorities finally were able to track down the people who were making the withdrawals.

After many false leads and dead ends, it became clear that the criminals were working for the Russian mafia. Calls arranging the transfers were traced, and eventually, a young Russian mathematician named Vladimir Levin was arrested for stealing a total of $12 million. Levin had created a network of calls that was so complex it could hardly be traced.

A cyberthief known as Maxus stole close to 300,000 credit card numbers from e-tailer CD Universe and demanded $100,000 in ransom. When the company denied him the money, Maxus posted the numbers on a public Web site. Authorities haven't been able to locate Maxus or verify the details of the crime, but it is possible that thousands of people lost full possession of their credit cards.

In 1995, an English hacker named Christopher Pile unleashed a virus designed to destroy data every Wednesday afternoon. One software company estimated that the virus cost them half a million English pounds ($730,000) in lost data. Pile served eighteen months in prison for his crime.

Convicted computer hacker Kevin Mitnick, *right*, is released from the Federal Correction Institute in Lompoc, California. A judge ordered him to stay away from computers for three years following his release from prison.

Kevin Mitnick first gained national attention when, as a teenager, he broke into a North American Air Defense Command computer. He also broke into the systems of telephone companies, which enabled him to listen in on private calls.

These pranks escalated to the invasion of MCI Communications' system, where Mitnick

read the e-mail of security professionals and learned how their computers and phone equipment were protected. Far from harmless, this feat cost the company $5 million and sent Mitnick to jail.

Believed to have a serious addiction to computer hacking, Mitnick later tapped into the California Department of Motor Vehicles' computer system to obtain driver's license records, and stole thousands of credit card numbers from some of Silicon Valley's best-known millionaires. Because he doesn't seem to have used these credit cards, or to have conducted any of his crimes for personal gain, authorities believe he is simply out to flaunt his technical skills.

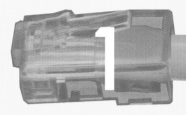

A Need for Internet Security

I n just a few years, the Internet revolution has turned the world on its head. The digital age, as it's sometimes called, has affected almost everyone. It has transformed the way people communicate. It has made the planet feel like a much smaller, more familiar place. Most of all, it has changed the way much of the world does business.

Business that is conducted electronically or over the Internet is known as electronic commerce— "e-commerce" for short. When people, companies, governments, or organizations do business using electronic technologies such as electronic mail (e-mail), Web sites, or computer connections, they are taking part in the world of e-commerce. Like the Internet, e-commerce has been around for quite some time—only in forms that you may not have recognized. Automatic teller machines (ATMs), for example, enable a form of e-commerce. ATMs allow bank customers to do business electronically. So do credit cards. They are an electronic connection to a credit card company, which electronically generates a bill.

E-commerce businesses replace what used to be paper-based work—requiring things like memos, paper bills, and paper money—with electronic work and communication among computers, fax machines, and phone and cable lines. For a company to do business in the digital age, there's no need to file piles of invoices and records. Everything can be stored on a computer. And if a customer wants to buy something, he or she can do it over the Internet—no need to even set foot in the store.

Today, thanks to e-commerce, business is conducted more quickly, inexpensively, and efficiently than ever before. And every day, the speed picks up, the efficiency improves, and new computers, software, and techniques are invented to make things more affordable. As the Internet revolution continues, more and more people are accepting the World Wide Web as a convenient and cost-efficient place to do business. Even as you read this, the world is rapidly changing. We're rushing headlong into a new era, a new millennium, a digital age.

WHY DO WE NEED TO BE SECURE?

From the look of things at the dawn of the twenty-first century, there's no end in sight to the worldwide explosion in electronic commerce. Experts predict that by 2004, the market for business-to-business (B2B) e-commerce—business conducted between two or more companies—will reach $2.7 trillion. At the same time, U.S. households will be spending more than $100 billion every year to buy a huge variety of products online, from CDs to cars to houses.

In order for e-commerce to flourish, however, it's necessary for e-businesses to collect vast amounts of information from one another and from consumers. Now, there's nothing wrong with sharing information. That's how business works. But when it comes to e-commerce, all that information flying around the digital highway presents a challenge. The electronic marketplace is nothing like the standard marketplace. In real-life, on-the-ground businesses, you can usually just walk right in the front door, talk to a person face-to-face, look at the product you want to buy, hand over the money, and walk out with your purchase.

On the Internet, however, it's not so easy. It can be hard to tell if an online store is for real. It's difficult to know if some businesses are scams designed to steal money from unknowing consumers. You can't be entirely sure that you can trust the people running the Web site. And when it comes time to give the business money—like when you decide to buy a CD with a credit card—you can't be sure the personal information on that credit card will even make it to the store.

One of the biggest challenges confronting the success of e-commerce is how to ensure that electronically conducted business, including the personal and financial information that must be shared for business to take place, is safe and secure. Just as you're never entirely safe when you carry cash in your pocket—it could be stolen—you're never entirely safe when you do business using digital technology. The Internet links information to millions of computers around the world. Any time information travels from one computer to another, it could potentially be stolen by a criminal. The digital world is a vast and complicated place, and many thieves take advantage of its anonymity.

Hackers are individuals who come up with ways to break into computer networks, often to steal confidential digital information. Hackers sometimes target corporate and government systems. But some steal credit card numbers and personal information such as

A laptop computer and software capable of modifying a cellular phone are the only tools some hackers need to break into computer networks.

passwords and social security numbers, and break into people's personal files. Sometimes they take information and use it to make money. Other times they just try to mess things up—like destroying important files stored in a government agency's computer.

With all the potential dangers that surround the digital business world, it should come as no surprise that e-commerce security is one of the hottest new fields in the world of computer science. E-commerce security professionals do everything they can to ensure that computer users remain safe from hackers and others who might try to steal or tamper with their private information. They develop protective software, build electronic barriers and fortresses, and keep up on the latest hacker "attacks" and techniques.

They use a technology called encryption to scramble digital information with secret codes and make it impossible to read as it travels between computers. They even build protective firewalls, designed as barriers between computers and criminals on the Internet. In fact, every day computer security professionals develop new ways to make e-commerce and electronic transactions safer and more secure. Their job is a tough one, sometimes involving long hours and challenging projects. But it's also an honorable one, as the very future of e-commerce—and the Internet—is in their hands.

HOME HACKERS

Home computer users who use a cable modem or a digital subscriber line (DSL) to connect to the Internet generally have nothing to complain about. After all, those types of connections are two of the world's fastest. They also allow Web surfers to stay online all the time without tying up their home phone lines. But cable and DSL connections do present one potential security issue—a vulnerability to hackers.

Here's the problem: Because an individual cable or DSL connection is part of a network of connections, and those connections are always on, it's easy for a computer hacker to sneak from his or her own computer into that of someone else in the network.

> "It's very easy for a 'company' to create a presence on the Web, sell things under false pretenses, and then close up shop and disappear."
>
> —*Steve Salter, director of the Better Business Bureau Online's reliability program*

People who dial up their Internet provider with a modem don't generally have this security problem because they hang up and disconnect when they're not surfing. It's kind of like shutting and locking the door to your house when you go to sleep as opposed to leaving it open all night long.

Fortunately, most cable and DSL providers recognize this security threat and do all that they can to discourage unauthorized intruders. Specially trained technicians go to their subscribers' homes and adjust their computer settings to make them less vulnerable to attacks. Or, if the adjustments are easy to make, they give their customers all the information they need to do it themselves. Another way cable and DSL providers protect their clients is through encryption. They make sure that all data transported on their lines is encrypted (put into code) and, hopefully, indecipherable to hackers.

Many computer users with high-speed connections or even modem-based connections take security one step further. Most install virus-protection software. And now, as the technology becomes easier to use, some also add the latest in intruder-blocking firewalls.

As hacker-repelling software, hardware, and encryption become more effective, home computer users with cable or DSL connections will have less and less to worry about. For now, however, there is a constant threat of intrusion. All surfers can do is keep posted on the latest technology and stay on guard.

Types of Security and Encryption

E-commerce security professionals do everything they can to make sure the business that takes place online is safe. Most security pros are computer science experts well-trained in programming, software and hardware design, and engineering. They use many different technologies to do their jobs effectively, and often they must invent new technologies as the world of e-commerce changes. They call these new inventions "leading-edge" technologies.

One of the most common leading-edge technologies that computer scientists use to protect e-commerce is encryption. Encryption has become so common in everyday online business that consumers often don't even realize they're using it.

Encryption is used to protect information as it travels between computers. When a digital consumer visits a Web page that asks for personal or financial information, that information is encrypted to keep third parties, like hackers, from seeing it. Banks use encryption techniques to ensure that account information is secure. Because encrypted messages can be decrypted only by someone on the other end, encryption guarantees that you're doing business with the bank (and only the bank) when you send it information through its site. You can tell the information you're sending is encrypted when you see a closed padlock symbol on your computer screen.

PUBLIC KEY ENCRYPTION

A company called Netscape Corporation invented one of the best-known encryption-security technologies. Secure Sockets Layer, or SSL, is a way for computers to make a secure connection to a server. Secure server connections are very important. Servers enable businesses and consumers to connect and buy and sell products online. If businesses aren't protected from intruders, consumers will be afraid to use them and be reluctant to hand over their credit card numbers. Likewise, businesses will be reluctant to set up shop on the Internet. SSL uses a strong coding method called public key encryption to put information in indecipherable code as it travels over the Internet. It's easy to tell when a Web site uses the SSL protocol—just look at the URL. If it starts with "https" instead of "http," the site is protected by SSL.

Public key encryption is a fairly new and very complex technology. A key is a string of symbols applied to an electronically transmitted message that makes the message unreadable while it travels between computers. Each party in a public key transaction has a "key pair." The key pair consists of two keys. The encryption process, which uses one of the two keys, is unprotected and available to the public. But part of the decryption process is secret, and only the other key in the pair can complete that process. Public key cryptography allows both parties in an electronic business transaction to positively identify each other and prove that they are who they say they are. It prevents a third party from eavesdropping or accessing the information. Of course, when you use public key encryption, you don't have to worry about these details—they're for the computer scientists to think about. All you have to do is click your mouse.

FIREWALLS

Another effective way to block intruders from accessing private information is through firewall technology. Firewalls are computers that stand like a protective wall between networks. For example, a company might place a firewall between its internal computer network and the Internet. All information traveling from the Internet to the company, and everything transmitted from the company over the Internet, must first pass through the firewall. It's like having an electronic guard. Firewalls control exactly what information can and cannot pass between the two networks.

AUTHENTICATION SECURITY

There are many other security technologies in addition to encryption and firewalls. For example, Web sites often require users to log on with a password. This is called authentication security. If the person types in the correct password, he or she is allowed to continue and is officially logged on. The Web site recognizes the password and determines that the person who typed it is not using a false identity.

Company workers also use passwords. Employees often use passwords to log on to their workstations or their company's network. They might have to enter another password to check their e-mail or surf the Internet. They may even have to enter a password to get into a particular division of the company to work on a specific project.

One problem with passwords is the fact that many people have trouble memorizing them. So instead of inventing new passwords every time they need one, they use the same password everywhere. Or they use easily guessed passwords, like their name, initials, or phone number. Or they write their passwords down. That makes it easy for someone to steal a person's password and get into a digital world where he or she is not supposed to be.

A new sort of "password," but safer, is a token. Tokens are cards that display a number that changes every few seconds. When logging on, the user must type in the number that is displayed on the token before it changes. That way the number acts like a password, but is used only once. Smart cards also act like passwords. Each smart card contains a unique code and other information that identifies its owner. When the owner plugs his or her card into a special computer slot, he or she is identified quickly and easily.

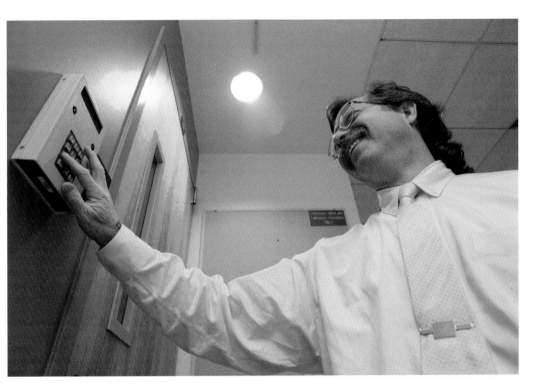

San Jose State University professor James L. Wayman, an expert on biometrics, demonstrates a device that uses face recognition software to allow entry to his lab.

BIOMETRICS AND VOICEPRINTS

Many other security systems are used in e-commerce, and most involve some sort of encryption process. But the future of e-commerce security may be in a field called biometrics. Biometric technology uses a physical characteristic of a person to uniquely identify that person. That physical characteristic might be your fingerprint, or maybe a unique pattern on your eyeball. No one else in the world has that fingerprint or eyeball pattern, so no one else can access the secret information. Voiceprints are similar to biometrics. The user says something and the computer recognizes his or her voice. Only then can the user access the private information on his or her computer.

Encryption, biometrics, passwords, smart cards— you name it, someone in the e-commerce security field invented it and someone else is working to improve it. Technology is constantly evolving, and e-commerce security must also evolve to keep up with the times. As sure as the Internet is changing the way the world does business, security experts are out there working hard to invent the next "ultimate" defense.

Sign Here, Please

E-commerce has had to get very creative with signatures. Because e-commerce is often conducted on a global scale—with one party in a transaction sometimes thousands of miles from the other—signing on the dotted line is not always easy. Until recently, in fact, in order for an e-commerce contract to be legally valid, the important paperwork often had to be printed out and mailed to the consumer for a regular ink-on-paper signature. The consumer would sign the documents, pop everything back in the mail, and the transaction could take place. There was one word for it: slow.

President Clinton demonstrates a smart card that allows electronic signatures. Clinton signed a bill giving an online "John Hancock" the same legal validity as a signature in pen and ink.

On October 1, 2000, however, that changed. On that day, a new law signed by President Bill Clinton made electronic "e-signatures" just as valid as regular signatures. Known as the Electronic Signatures in Global Commerce Act, the law cleared the way for a whole new method of doing business in the digital age.

The definition of an e-signature depends on whom you ask, and for now there are many different kinds of digital signatures. An e-security company called Interlink Electronics invented something called an

Interlink Electronics invented the ePad, a small electronic pad that links to a computer, which keeps track of package deliveries. When a package is delivered, the recipient signs his or her name with a special pen that records and stores the signature in a main computer.

ePad, a small electronic pad that links to a computer. Using a special pen, a person can sign his or her name on the pad's surface. The details of that signature, including every little bump and squiggle and even the speed at which it's written, are captured by the pad and sent directly to the computer for storage. When that same person signs his or her name in the future, security is guaranteed because the computer record makes it easy to verify the signature.

Other forms of e-signatures that might become common in the future include things that bear no resemblance whatsoever to traditional signatures. Biological verification systems like retina scans or fingerprinting might work. Or maybe some form of DNA identification will be available in the future. Encryption will likely be popular, too, using scrambled numbers and letters and other symbols to identify the "right" people and keep out the "wrong."

Ultimately, the legal acceptance of e-signatures means e-commerce will become faster, less expensive, more convenient, and much safer. There will be less paperwork and no need for time-consuming mailing. And with an easy-to-identify code or signature, it will be much more difficult for criminals to commit fraud or steal innocent people's private information by pretending to be someone they aren't.

CUTTING-EDGE ENCRYPTION

When it comes to computer systems security, the U.S. government does not mess around. There are military secrets to protect. Financial systems must be guarded. Electronic communications between high-ranking officials must take place in absolute privacy, without the threat of hackers or spies tapping in.

Over the years, the government has turned to the latest in encryption technology to protect its sensitive electronic information. Encryption uses complex mathematical formulas to scramble messages as they travel from one computer to another. Once the message reaches its destination, it is unscrambled so it can be read. As computer scientists invent new code-making techniques, encryption standards change, so the government must periodically update its systems. When they do, they declare a new "standard"—the encryption technique that all government agencies must use. In 1977, for example, the National Institute of Standards and Technology, or NIST, an agency of the U.S. Commerce Department's Technology Administration, adopted what it called the Data Encryption Standard (DES).

The strength of any encryption technique is usually determined by the length and complexity of the mathematical formula that it uses. The DES code is incredibly complex—for a computer to break the code, it has to run through nearly 720 quadrillion combinations (720 followed by 15 zeros).

Until a few years ago, such a huge number of combinations made the DES code impossible to break. The government used it without any serious problems. Private companies used the publicly available code to safely protect things like financial transactions. In fact, even today there are hundreds of encryption products that use DES or a special variation of DES to protect everything from ATM and credit card transactions to Internet purchases to e-mails. But now computers are much more powerful than they once were, and specialized "DES-cracking" hardware—run by sophisticated hackers—can break the code quickly and easily.

With the security of the government at stake, in 1997 the NIST decided it was time for a new standard. But they had a problem: How could they ensure that the new encryption standard they developed was the best one for the job—one that was

Company Profile

Company: CyberGuard Corp.

Headquarters: Fort Lauderdale, Florida

Web site: www.cyberguard.com

Founded: 1996

Employees: Approximately eighty

Mission: "To give organizations worldwide the power to safeguard vital data through network security solutions."

Key product: CyberGuard Firewall, a multilevel secure computer that stands between internal networks—or between an internal network and the Internet—to provide a single secure connection point through which all data must travel. The firewall restricts access to information based on the sensitivity of the information and the access authorization of system users.

fast and easy to use, yet could stand up to the threat of hackers for many years to come? Their solution: Stage a competition.

The NIST invited top-notch researchers from all over the world to submit their best data-encryption formulas for evaluation. The idea was to sift through the entries and pick out the one formula that outdid all the others. The one that was most secure, fastest, and versatile would win the competition and become the government's all-new Advanced Encryption Standard, or AES.

Finally, on October 2, 2000, three years after the competition began, the NIST picked a winner: Rijndael. Rijndael (pronounced "rhine-doll") is the invention of two Belgian computer scientists named Vincent Rijmen and Joan Daemen. Dr. Rijmen, a postdoctoral researcher in the electrical engineering department of Katholieke Universiteit Leuven, and Dr. Daemen, who works with a group called Proton World International, are internationally recognized experts in cryptography.

Rijndael, which is available for anyone to use, whether he or she is with the government or in a private business, makes the DES look like a high school science project. Today's computers have no chance whatsoever of cracking it. The NIST estimates it would take almost 149 trillion years to decrypt a message sent using the Rijndael system. If you thought the DES's 720 quadrillion combinations were a lot, think again. Rijndael is so sophisticated that hackers will have to use up to 1,100,000,000,000,000,000,000,000,000,000,000,000,000, 000,000,000,000,000,000,000,000,000,000,000,000,000 combinations to crack it. Experts think it will be at least several decades before computers are powerful enough to break the code.

The NIST plans to officially adopt the AES in the spring of 2001. Once Rijndael is approved as the new standard, it will be used by U.S. government agencies to protect their sensitive information.

"[The Advanced Encryption Standard] will serve as a critical computer security tool supporting the rapid growth of electronic commerce. This is a very significant step toward creating a more secure digital economy. It will allow e-commerce and e-government to flourish safely, creating new opportunities for all Americans."

—*U.S. secretary of commerce,*
Norman Y. Mineta

Other nations around the world are also likely to use the code. And private businesses, too, will certainly use this powerful formula in their latest security software. In fact, it's only a matter of time before the AES becomes not only the government standard, but also the world standard in encryption technology. For more information on the Advanced Encryption Standard, visit the Computer Security Resource Center of the NIST at www.nist.gov/aes.

Careers in Security and Encryption

s more and more people use the Internet, and as e-commerce continues to grow, the need for ambitious and highly skilled e-commerce security professionals will also expand. There are dozens of well-respected companies around the world that specialize in e-commerce security. There are also many young, motivated, and exceedingly smart computer experts who are setting out on their own, starting new businesses and inventing new products. They're the entrepreneurs of the technology age, working to make e-commerce safe for businesses and consumers.

E-commerce security experts work with the latest technologies in a field that didn't exist a few years ago. They're an important part of the digital revolution, focused on personal growth and success, but also on the success of the companies for which they work. The world of computers and electronic communications is extremely fast paced, so if you decide on a career in e-commerce security, you will never be bored. Every day you'll have new challenges and new projects.

If you work for the right company, you'll get great pay and benefits. You'll work long, hard hours, but you'll also be rewarded with vacations and time off. You may be able to work from home sometimes as a "telecommuter." Telecommuters can do their work from the comfort of a home office. You may get stock options, which give you part ownership of your company and give you the incentive to help make it grow and succeed. If your company is truly leading edge, it may help train you in new technologies by sending you to conferences and professional meetings or helping you pay for courses in the latest security techniques. You'll be promoted as you achieve your goals, rewarded for your talents, and pushed to your full potential. That's the way business works in the digital age—whether you're self-employed or part of a large global company, you must push the limits of the field in order to stay ahead of the competition.

E-commerce security professionals invent, design, develop, build, and market security products

Software engineers are in high demand in the field of e-commerce security. They work to develop new security products and update existing software programs to make them more effective.

that help e-businesses and digital consumers inter-
act without threat of external attacks or fraud.
Most of those on the front line who actually create
software that encrypts messages or firewall hardware that blocks intruders are computer science
experts. They create technologies found in Web
browsers, servers, e-mail systems, and networks.

RESEARCH SCIENTISTS

Research scientists work to develop new cryptography and security technologies. They serve as team
leaders on some projects. To be a research scientist
you must have experience in the cryptography
field. You must also have technical writing and professional presentation skills—the kinds of skills
required to explain complex subjects to regular
people. You must be a great problem solver—the
kind who loves difficult puzzles and challenging
games. You have to be open-minded, professional,
attentive, dynamic, and enthusiastic about working
together with other professionals as a team. Often
you need a master's degree or even a Ph.D. in
computer science or mathematics.

SOFTWARE ENGINEERS

Software engineers are in high demand in the field of e-commerce security. Like research scientists, they work to develop new and innovative security products. They also update existing software programs with new features to make them more effective. Software engineers need very strong programming skills, and most have at least a bachelor's degree in computer science.

SECURITY CONSULTANTS

Security consultants work to design security products, but they also work directly with consumers and other businesses. They travel to businesses to look at their computer network structures and determine what security devices are necessary to ensure safe and secure working environments. They consult with others in the e-commerce world about what they can do to make their businesses secure. In addition to needing a thorough understanding of computer programs, security consultants need excellent communication skills. Also, they have to like the road—they spend much of their time traveling around the world.

ROUNDING OUT THE TEAM

Other e-commerce security jobs include those you might not think have anything to do with security. Most e-security companies, for example, need a whole team of people—not just computer experts, but also other pros in accounting, human resources, marketing, and sales. These people are necessary for an e-commerce security business to function.

Application support/programmers work to develop and support systems that are needed to solve everyday business problems. They write reports, suggest solutions, and help the various departments in a business work together and run smoothly.

"E-commerce security requires constant work on the leading edge of Internet and computer technologies. My job provides me with an excellent opportunity for this. The security field has multitudes of opportunities in various fields within it. There are careers in developing computer virus detectors, information warfare protection, cryptography, distributed secure computing, new user identification techniques involving biometrics, development of secure network protocols, improved firewalls, and many other technologies."

—E-commerce security professional

Help Wanted

Here's a job announcement from a leading e-commerce security firm. Do you have the skills for the job?

Entry-Level Software Engineer Requirements and Responsibilities:

▶ Versioning (making new and old software versions compatible with one another)
▶ Installation tools and online installation
▶ Java help
▶ Java development and testing requirements
▶ B.S. or M.S. in computer science or equivalent
▶ OOD/OOP (object-oriented design/object-oriented programming)
▶ Java client/server experience
▶ Strong problem solving, debugging, and communication skills
▶ Team player considered a plus
▶ Knowledge or experience with network/Internet security concepts, such as firewalls, authentication, auditing, etc.

Software quality-assurance engineers make sure software works the way it's supposed to work. The people in human resources sift through piles of applicants and hire the right people necessary to make the company grow. Those in marketing figure out ways to make products attractive to consumers.

Accountants keep track of money and make sure the business is profitable. Customer relations and technical-support specialists help customers when they have questions and explain complex issues in order to solve problems.

The fact is, when it comes down to the nuts and bolts of business management and what makes a business successful, e-commerce security is a lot like any other field. With a talented workforce, motivated individuals, and a top-of-the-line team, any e-security business is bound to do well.

Getting Started in a Career in Security and Encryption

If you are an expert problem solver, love mathematics, and are fascinated with the challenge of creating computer software or codes, a job in security and encryption might be for you.

If you want to get started in the security and encryption field, ask those already in the business to tell you about their jobs. Talk to your teachers or parents to see if they know anyone in the field. If they do, try to schedule a time when you can meet the person, maybe even visit him or her on the job. If no one knows an e-commerce security professional, see if you can find one through the Internet. Go to the Web site of an e-commerce security company and find the staff e-mail addresses. E-mail staff members and ask if it would be all right to talk about their jobs and take a "virtual" tour of their career.

Ask those in the field what they like about their jobs. Find out what they don't like and why. Ask them to tell you everything they can to help you decide whether a career in e-commerce security is really for you.

"My entry into network security was a progressive path in my career. After graduating from college with a computer science degree, I entered the computer programming profession doing operating system development. This gave me a unique insight into the internals of computer systems and their operation. While working on operating systems, I became interested in network subsystems within the operating system. This led to more work on network protocols and network devices. Eventually, I became involved in the development of a cryptographic network used to 'hide' network packets within other network packets. This product was incorporated into our firewall product, and thus, my entry into the world of e-commerce security was 'secured.' "

—*John Ryker, E-commerce security*

HOW TO PREPARE

Once you've made up your mind to become an e-commerce security professional, it's time to focus on the qualifications you need to get the job. As a high school student, it's very important to get good grades

If you want to become an e-commerce security professional, take computer and math courses in high school. In college, you should major in computer science.

in all subjects so you can go to a good college. Try to take computer classes, of course, but also take as many math and English classes as you can.

In college, you should major in computer science. As a computer science student, you'll learn all about how computers work, what they can do, and how to program them to do specific things. You'll also take math, physics, and electronics courses. If you think you might want to start your own e-commerce security business someday, you should also take classes in business, economics, and management, as well as other classes that cover the ins and outs of running your own company.

Before you graduate from college, get some work experience. You can do this through an internship. An internship allows you to work and learn at the same time. Companies like to hire former interns right out of college because they have on-the-job experience. You don't necessarily have to have any qualifications to be an intern, just a desire to learn. You may not be paid very well, or at all, but you will gain valuable experience that will help in the future. You also might establish connections in the e-commerce security field that you can use later when it comes time to get a real job. There is plenty of information about internship

Hit the Links

The Internet is home to so many sites devoted to security and encryption, it's tough to weed through them all and find the best. Fortunately, some sites have already done that job for you. A cryptography company called Counterpane Internet Security, for example, provides an extensive list of "Crypto Links" on its Web site at www.counterpane.com/hotlist.html. The list includes cryptography companies, universities with cryptography programs, specific university courses in cryptography, and many other useful sites and sources of cryptographic information. The National Institutes of Health Center for Information Technology maintains another good security site at www.cit.nih.gov/home.asp.

programs on the Internet. Try checking out www.internshipprograms.com or www.techaccess.org. Corporations such as IBM and Dell also offer internships.

Many security professionals go on to graduate school to study computer science or computer engineering. Some even go to business school, where they learn how to start a new company. They learn the finer details of the general subjects they were taught in college, and by the time they graduate with a master's degree or Ph.D., they're fully prepared to begin a career.

According to those currently in the field, one of the most important characteristics of an e-commerce pro is the ability to think on your feet. You not only have to know how to do your job as a computer expert, but you also have to think like a customer and consider why, how, and where your product will be useful. You need general programming experience, but you also must understand networking, network devices, and network layouts. You have to know how computers work together, not just how computers work.

Finally, you need to have great teamwork skills. Here's how one security pro sees it:

"Although I'm a manager of a team of engineers, I am a member of that team. When our team works together to provide solutions, everyone wins. We compensate for each other's weaknesses, yet we accelerate our learning curve by sharing ideas and speed up our time to market by sharing the workload. There is a great satisfaction when your team completes a project by developing a good, sound product that the customer wants."

The truth is, an e-commerce security career is one in which the education and training never really end. You're constantly learning new techniques and developing new products. On-the-job training is common. You'll attend seminars and lectures all over the country, perhaps all over the world. In fact, you'll probably continue learning new things until you retire.

BACK TO SCHOOL

As the Internet grows in popularity, and millions of new users go online every year, the need for well-trained security and encryption professionals becomes more and more apparent. In the past, a security company could require only that job applicants have computer-related experience or a degree in computer science. Often, applicants had no encryption experience whatsoever—they had to get that experience and learn new techniques on the job.

Today that's no longer the case. Now young people interested in careers in Internet security and encryption can get experience before they ever land their first job. Many of the world's top universities offer specialized programs of study in security and encryption technologies. At Syracuse University in New York, for example, students in the school's Center for Business Information Technologies can enroll in the Webmaster-Website Administrator Program. In a course called Building Internet/Intranet Security, students tackle network

"E-commerce security requires constant work on the leading edge of Internet and computer technologies. You have to be able to 'think outside of the box.' You have to try to think like an engineer, but at the same time get into the mind of a malicious user and step back and look at your software design for weaknesses . . . E-commerce security must work in order for the Internet to work. One cannot exist without the other."

—David Rhein, manager of security software, CyberGuard Corporation

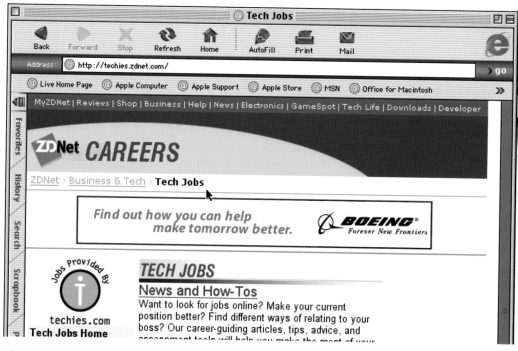

There are many resources available on the Internet to assist you in your job search.

security issues and learn all the latest technologies and techniques that Internet corporations use to keep their sites and consumers safe. They learn how to discourage hackers, prevent data theft, and fend off intruders.

A company called Global Knowledge (www.am.globalknowledge.com) also provides training for current and future e-security professionals in the United States and Canada. Fully embracing the Internet revolution, they offer courses that can be taken online in addition to traditional classroom-based courses. Their Network Security and Firewall Administration course, for example, teaches students how intruders attack and how to counter those attacks. It shows them how to build a security plan, set up a firewall system, and protect a host server. The course even includes hands-on labs to give students practice for the real thing.

It's only a matter of time before universities begin offering complete undergraduate and graduate degrees in Internet security. The field is becoming so large and complex that highly trained individuals are needed right out of college. For hackers and criminals, of course, the prospect of having to deal with a yearly fleet of well-educated security experts is incredibly bad news. But for those interested in protecting the future of e-commerce, times couldn't be better.

FINDING THE JOB

Finding a job in the e-commerce security world can be a daunting task. Fortunately, though, good workers are in high demand. If you have the right qualifications, you're bound to land a good position.

When you are ready to look for work, you'll probably start with your résumé. Tailor it to the type of job you want, stressing your strengths and interests. If you need help with your résumé, talk to professionals in the field and ask them for tips. Professional résumé-writing services are also available in many areas.

Once you have your résumé in order, it's time to post it. Thanks to the Internet, doing so is easy. Go to Web-based job-finding services like monster.com, jobs.com, wetfeet.com, hotjobs.com, and guru.com and show your résumé to prospective employers. Or go to a site with tech jobs, such as www.techies.zdnet.com, where you can search for high-tech jobs on their search engine.

Another good place to look for work on the Web is at company sites. Most e-commerce security businesses list open positions on their home pages and explain everything you need to know to apply. Happy surfing!

STARTING YOUR OWN SECURITY AND ENCRYPTION BUSINESS

E-entrepreneurs—those who are starting their own Internet-based businesses and leading the

Company Profile

Company: VeriSign, Inc.

Headquarters: Mountain View, California

Web site: www.verisign.com

Founded: 1995

Employees: Approximately 300

Mission: "To provide public key infra-structure (PKI) and digital certificate solutions to enable trusted commerce and communications over private and public networks."

Key product: VeriSign Wireless Server IDs, used by Web site developers and wireless service providers to protect confidential information such as credit card numbers, online forms, and financial data from interception and hacking.

e-commerce movement—are among the most highly motivated and talented professionals in the world today. Their jobs are not easy. They must take what they know best (for instance, e-commerce security) and figure out a way to design a profitable business around it.

If you think you might want to start your own e-commerce security business someday, one of the first things you should do is talk to other entrepreneurs. Learn from their mistakes so you won't have to make them yourself. Find out what they did right and wrong. Take notes. Then, when you're ready, analyze everything and figure out how you can do better in your own business.

One key component of creating a new e-commerce business is getting the right people to help you do the job. You'll want to hire highly qualified individuals that you can trust to work hard and make the business succeed. Surround yourself with smart, ambitious workers, and your business just might take off.

Finally, you'll have to deal with the nuts and bolts of operating a business. You'll have to rent or buy a building to house your software and hardware. You might need trucks for shipping products. You'll need an accountant to help you with your money and make sure that you pay all the right taxes. The logistics of creating and running a new business can be overwhelming. But if you've got the drive, there's no limit to how far you can go.

Computers, computer networks, and the millions of people who use them to communicate are a major part of what it means to do business. If we don't live in an entirely digital economy just yet, we certainly will in the future. But with the arrival of the Internet and e-business, the need for cutting-edge security technology has also arrived. As more and more people and businesses digitally connect, the opportunity for criminals to interfere with everyday business affairs also increases. E-security and those who choose to devote their lives to it are absolutely critical to the continued success of the Internet and the power it has held in transforming the world.

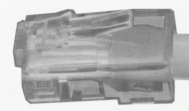

Glossary

attack An attempt to get around the security controls on a computer to do something not normally permitted, like steal private information.

authenticate To determine that computer users are who they say they are.

authentication key A sequence of numbers, letters, and other characters used to identify the sender in an online transaction and to ensure that data sent in that transaction is safe.

biometrics The use of physical characteristics such as fingerprints, eye patterns, or DNA to identify a computer user.

B2B e-commerce "Business-to-business" e-commerce; buying and selling between online businesses.

cryptography   Secret, coded writing used to disguise transactions or communications between computer users.

data   Information.

Data Encryption Standard (DES)   A cryptographic code used to protect sensitive information and approved in 1977 by the U.S. government's National Institute of Standards and Technology.

decrypt   To decipher information that is written in code.

digital consumer   One who shops on the Internet.

digital signature   The digital equivalent of a written signature; a unique digital code that identifies the sender of a message.

e-commerce   Business that takes place electronically or on the Internet.

e-mail   Short for electronic mail; a way to send messages from one computer to another.

encrypt   To put into code.

encryption   The process of putting something into code to ensure security and privacy while it's transmitted between computers.

firewall   A computer system or combination of systems designed to protect a personal computer or computer network from intruders on the Internet.

hacker   An unauthorized person who tries to get by security barriers on a computer system.

Internet   The world's largest computer "internetwork," made up of many smaller networks or computers electronically linked together.

Java   A programming language developed by Sun Microsystems.

key   A string of symbols applied to electronically transmitted text in order to make it unreadable while it's transmitted between computers.

network   Two or more connected computers that can communicate with one another.

programmer   A person who writes computer programs.

protocol   A common language that computers use to communicate and exchange information.

public key cryptography   Cryptography in which the encryption process is unprotected and available to the public, but part of the decryption process is secret. It ensures security by only allowing someone who knows both parts of the decryption process to decode an encrypted message.

Secure Sockets Layer (SSL)   A protocol that
creates a secure connection and encrypts information as it travels over the Internet.

software   Programs designed for use with computers.

virus   A computer program that can make copies
of itself and attach itself to other programs,
sometimes with harmful effects.

voiceprint   A way for computers to allow access
using voice recognition.

World Wide Web   Interconnected files and sites
on the Internet, accessible through a browser.

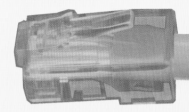

For More Information

Carnegie Mellon Software Engineering
Institute's CERT Coordination Center
http://www.cert.org

Computer Incident Advisory Capability
(CIAC) Notes
http://www.ciac.org/ciac

GuardCentral.com
http://www.guardcentral.com

Information Systems Security
Association (ISSA)
7044 South 13th Street
Oak Creek, WI 53154
(414) 768-8000
http://www.issa-intl.org

International Association for Cryptologic
    Research (IACR)
IACR General Secretariat
Santa Rosa Administrative Center
University of California
Santa Barbara, CA 93106-6120
http://www.iacr.org

National Security Agency, Information
    Systems Security Organization
9800 Savage Road, Suite 6779
Fort Meade, MD 20755-6779
(800) 688-6115
http://www.nsa.gov/isso/index.html

National Security Telecommunications and
    Information Systems Security Committee
http://www.nstissc.gov/html/flashed_index.html

Security News Links
http://www.securitynews.org

System Administration, Networking, and
    Security (SANS) Institute Online
(301) 951-0102
http://www.sans.org

For Further Reading

Cameron, Debra. *E-Commerce Security Strategies: Protecting the Enterprise.* Charleston, SC: Computer Technology Research Corporation, 1998.

Ford, Warwick, and Michael S. Baum. *Secure Electronic Commerce: Building the Infrastructure for Digital Signatures and Encryption.* Upper Saddle River, NJ: Prentice Hall, 1997.

Ghosh, Anup K. *E-Commerce Security: Weak Links, Best Defenses.* New York: John Wiley and Sons, 1998.

Hassler, Vesna. *Security Fundamentals for E-Commerce.* Boston, MA: Artech House, 2001.

Knittel, John, and Michael Soto. *Everything You Need to Know About the Dangers of Computer Hacking.* New York: The Rosen Publishing Group, Inc., 2000.

Sexton, Conor. *E-Commerce and Security*. Woburn, MA: Butterworth-Heinemann, 2001.

Smith, Rob. *The Complete Idiot's Guide to E-Commerce.* Indianapolis, IN: Que Education and Training, 2000.

MAGAZINES AND ELECTRONIC PUBLICATIONS

Cipher
http://www.ieee-security.org/cipher.html

Computer Security News Daily
http://www.mountainwave.com

Internet Security Advisor
http://www.advisor.com/wHome.nsf/wPages/Samain

Netsurfer Focus
http://www.netsurf.com/nsf

SC Magazine
http://www.scmagazine.com

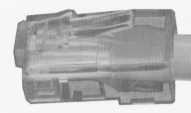

Index

ABOUT THE AUTHOR

Chris Hayhurst is a freelance writer living in Colorado.

PHOTO CREDITS

Pp. 6, 21, 23, 24, 34 © AP Photo World Wide; p. 12 © AP Photo/*Los Angeles Daily News*; p. 42 © Michael S. Yamashita/Corbis; p. 48 © zdnet careers.com.

SERIES DESIGN AND LAYOUT

Les Kanturek